◄I'M GOING TO BE A►

Fire Fighter

◄ I'M GOING TO BE A ►

Fire Fighter

by Edith Kunhardt

The author thanks Harry, Donna, Holly, Lisa, and Emily Halsey of Bridgehampton, N.Y., for their generous help and patience during this project. Many thanks also to the members of the Bridgehampton Fire Department for their invaluable assistance, especially to John "Red" White, Jimmy Walker, and Pete Garypie.

Library of Congress Cataloging-in-Publication Data available.

ISBN 0-590-25483-9

Copyright © 1989 by Edith Kunhardt.
All rights reserved. Published by Scholastic Inc.
CARTWHEEL BOOKS and the CARTWHEEL BOOKS logo are registered trademarks of Scholastic Inc.

12 11   3 4 5/0

Printed in the U.S.A.   23
First Scholastic printing, October 1995

SCHOLASTIC INC.
New York   Toronto   London   Auckland   Sydney

My name is Holly. I'm at the firehouse.
This is my dad. He is a volunteer fire fighter.
That means he isn't a fire fighter all the time.
He works at another job. When there is a fire,
he leaves his job and rushes to put the fire out.
I want to be a fire fighter, too.

Look! Daddy is bringing out the truck!

My mom and my little sisters, Lisa and Emily, watch. The engine makes a big noise. We all get a little scared.

Dad turns off the engine
and puts on the brake.

We climb onto the truck. This is a pumper truck. It carries many coiled-up hoses. It pumps water onto the fire.

The hoses attach to shiny valves.

Dad wears a radio on his belt so that, wherever he is, he can hear if there's a fire.

Dad shows me a pike pole, an ax, and a pry bar. These tools help fire fighters get inside a burning house or car.

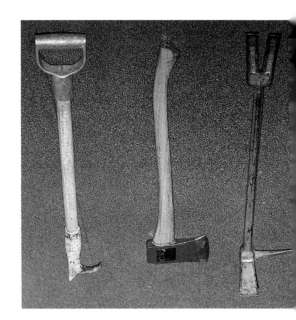

Dad carries his turnout gear in his truck. His boots, coat, and helmet are in a red bag inside a box. Extra turnout uniforms are kept on the fire truck.

Dad tries on his turnout uniform.

Then Lisa and I try it on.

At home we practice what to do if there is a fire. We crawl on the floor, where the smoke is less thick. We feel the door to see if it is hot. If it is hot, we don't open the door because there might be fire on the other side.

We escape out a window. Thank goodness this window is on the first floor!

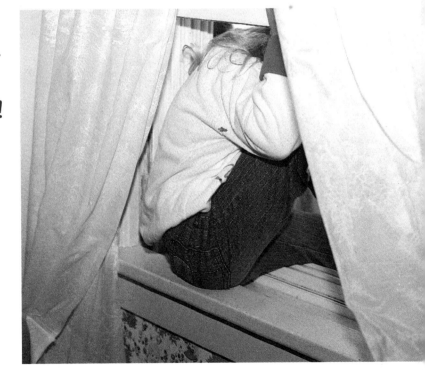

We decide ahead of time where to meet
outside the house. Our family meeting place
is under this tree.

One night a voice on Daddy's radio says there is a fire! The voice tells exactly where the fire is. Daddy gets the keys to his truck and runs out the door. He drives straight to the fire.

At the same time, other volunteer fire fighters leave their homes and jobs. They rush to the firehouse. They jump into a fire truck and drive to the fire.

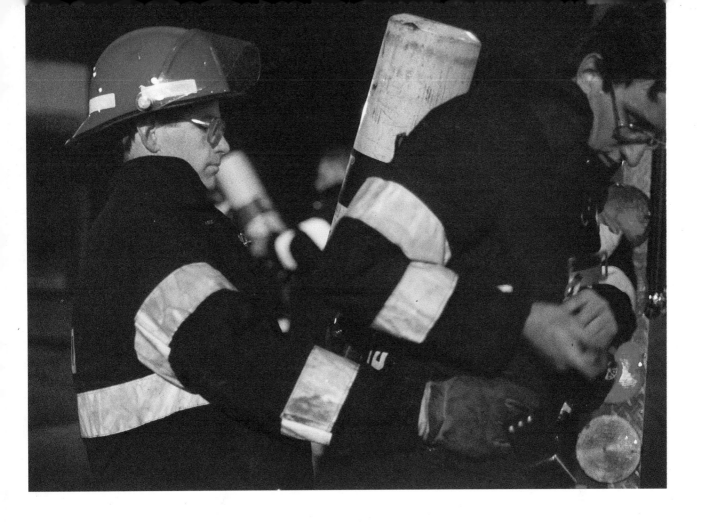

The fire is in a store. Daddy puts on his turnout uniform. He helps another fire fighter put on an oxygen tank. With the tank and a mask, the fire fighter will be able to breathe if he goes into the store.

The fire fighters attach hoses to the pumper truck. They spray water onto the fire.

The fire is out. No one is hurt. There was no one in the store.

Dad coils up a hose.

The fire fighters put their equipment in their truck.

They drive back to the firehouse. "Good night,"
they say. They're tired. They've done a good job.

The next morning we have breakfast.

Dad gets up late. When he joins us at the breakfast table, he tells us about the fire. He shows us how the flames shot up in the air. My dad is brave.

After breakfast, Lisa and Emily and I go out to play. Can you guess what we play?

I'm going to be a fire fighter.